The United Nations
Leadership and Challenges in a Global World

Cultural Globalization and
Celebrating Diversity

The United Nations:
Leadership and Challenges in a Global World

The United Nations
Leadership and Challenges in a Global World

Cultural Globalization and Celebrating Diversity

Sheila Nelson

SERIES ADVISOR
Bruce Russett

Mason Crest Publishers
Philadelphia

Mason Crest
450 Parkway Drive, Suite D
Broomall, PA 19008
www.masoncrest.com

Printed and bound in the United States of America.

First printing
9 8 7 6 5 4 3 2 1

Series ISBN: 978-1-4222-3427-3
ISBN: 978-1-4222-3429-7
ebook ISBN: 978-1-4222-8543-5

Library of Congress Cataloging-in-Publication Data
on file

Design by Sherry Williams and Tilman Reitzle, Oxygen Design Group.
Cover photos: Fotolia/Nobilior (top); Dollar Photo Club/Dmitriy Kalinin (bottom).

CONTENTS

KEY ICONS TO LOOK FOR:

 Words to Understand: These words with their easy-to-understand definitions will increase the reader's understanding of the text, while building vocabulary skills.

 Sidebars: This boxed material within the main text allows readers to build knowledge, gain insights, explore possibilities, and broaden their perspectives by weaving together additional information to provide realistic and holistic perspectives.

 Research Projects: Readers are pointed toward areas of further inquiry connected to each chapter. Suggestions are provided for projects that encourage deeper research and analysis.

 Text-Dependent Questions: These questions send the reader back to the text for more careful attention to the evidence presented there.

 Series Glossary of Key Terms: This back-of-the-book glossary contains terminology used throughout the series. Words found here increase the reader's ability to read and comprehend higher-level books and articles in this field.

INTRODUCTION

by Dr. Bruce Russett

THE UNITED NATIONS WAS FOUNDED IN 1945 by the victors of World War II. They hoped the new organization could learn from the mistakes of the League of Nations that followed World War I—and prevent another war.

The United Nations has not been able to bring worldwide peace; that would be an unrealistic hope. But it has contributed in important ways to the world's experience of more than sixty years without a new world war. Despite its flaws, the United Nations has contributed to peace.

Like any big organization, the United Nations is composed of many separate units with different jobs. These units make three different kinds of contributions. The most obvious to students in North America and other democracies are those that can have a direct and immediate impact for peace.

Especially prominent is the Security Council, which is the only UN unit that can authorize the use of military force against countries and can require all UN members to cooperate in isolating an aggressor country's economy. In the Security Council, each of the big powers—Britain, China, France, Russia, and the United States—can veto any proposed action. That's because the founders of United Nations recognized that if the Council tried to take any military action against the strong opposition of a big power it would result in war. As a result, the United Nations was often sidelined during the Cold War era. Since the end of the Cold War in 1990, however, the Council has authorized many military actions, some directed against specific aggressors but most intended as more neutral peacekeeping efforts. Most of its peacekeeping efforts have been to end civil wars rather than wars between countries. Not all have succeeded, but many have. The United Nations Secretary-General also has had an important role in mediating some conflicts.

UN units that promote trade and economic development make a different kind of contribution. Some help to establish free markets for greater prosperity, or like the UN Development Programme, provide economic and technical assistance to reduce poverty in poor countries. Some are especially concerned with environmental problems or health issues. For example, the World Health Organization and UNICEF deserve great credit for eliminating the deadly disease of smallpox from the world. Poor countries especially support the United Nations for this reason. Since many wars, within and between countries, stem from economic deprivation, these efforts make an important indirect contribution to peace.

Still other units make a third contribution: they promote human rights. The High Commission for Refugees, for example, has worked to ease the distress of millions of refugees who have fled their countries to escape from war and political persecution. A special unit of the Secretary-General's office has supervised and assisted free elections in more than ninety countries. It tries to establish stable and democratic governments in newly independent countries or in countries where the people have defeated a dictatorial government. Other units promote the rights of women, children, and religious and ethnic minorities. The General Assembly provides a useful setting for debate on these and other issues.

These three kinds of action—to end violence, to reduce poverty, and to promote social and political justice—all make a contribution to peace. True peace requires all three, working together.

The UN does not always succeed: like individuals, it makes mistakes . . . and it often learns from its mistakes. Despite the United Nations' occasional stumbles, over the years it has grown and moved for-ward. These books will show you how.

The peoples of the world are more connected now than ever before, in large part due to the ease of air travel. Pictured here is the Ninoy Aquino airport in the Philippines.

CHAPTER ONE

What Is Globalization?

Have you ever heard people say, "It's a small world"? What do they mean by that? After all, the Earth is 24,902 miles (40,076 km) measured around the equator—which isn't exactly small.

Hundreds of years ago, people were not sure what lay on the other side of the world, or even if there was another side of the world. The Earth seemed like a vast and mysterious place. In the fifteenth century, explorers mapped out most of the globe, but travel to distant places took months. Communication was slow and uncertain. People in different parts of the world lived very different kinds of lives. They

 WORDS TO UNDERSTAND

diversity: variety.

exchange rates: rates at which money of one country is exchanged for the money of another.

forgery: the act of making or producing an illegal copy of something.

multiculturalism: existence of the cultures of different countries, ethnic groups, or religions.

piracy: illegally seizing property or people, including intellectual property.

spoke different languages, ate different foods, wore different clothes, and had different traditions.

As technology became more advanced, things such as transportation and communication became quicker and easier. Today, all someone needs to do to talk to people from around the world is pick up a phone or click on to a computer. Traveling halfway around the globe now takes hours instead of months, and is relatively safe.

Globalization describes the process of connecting different parts of the world. Sometimes a certain part of the world will be more affected

During the fifteenth century, European explorers reached the shores of the American continents, one milestone in the early process of connecting people from distant lands. This print shows Christopher Columbus saying goodbye to Spain's Queen Isabella at the start of his first voyage west in 1492, when he reached the Americas.

than others by these connections, and sometimes one type of connection will be strongly felt in an area while other types of connections are barely noticeable in that same area. An example would be during a war, when there are many military connections but not very many economic ones.

Cultural Globalization

The idea of globalization can be very complicated and involves many different aspects. The term "cultural globalization" refers to the effects of many different types of globalization taken together, such as trade and the flow of goods across international borders, technological advances leading to faster and better communication and travel between different parts of the world, and the spread of ideas across the globe. These things all work together. Travel and communication, for example, have become so much easier in the last century that knowledge about different parts of the world has drastically increased. This has led to an increased understanding about different cultures as well as a desire to improve trade and ties between nations.

Multiculturalism and cultural **diversity** also result from cultural globalization. Today in large cities you can find restaurants serving food from almost everywhere in the world. Grocery stores stock international foods as well. Music from dozens of different countries is available. Many cities have sections where most residents are from a certain part of the world—such as Chinatown or Little Italy. The people who live in these areas hold the traditional festivals of their native countries, eat traditional foods, and sometimes wear traditional clothing.

CHANGING WAYS OF LIFE

For many, globalization is a positive change bringing different cultures together and providing jobs to poor people. However, globalization can often change traditional ways of life by destroying languages and customs. Moreover, people can lose their jobs because products can be made more cheaply somewhere else.

Many cities across the globe have their own ethnic neighborhoods where residents can enjoy food of other cultures. Pictured here is a restaurant on Dolores Street in Mexico City's Chinatown in 2009.

Media and the Internet

American movies are shown across the world. Books by international writers are translated into dozens of languages and read by thousands of people. Independent filmmakers in Africa or the Middle East submit their works to international film festivals, offering glimpses into their world and life. The media have allowed people to see into other cultures, encouraging diversity and acceptance of worldwide differences. Some complain, however, that since it is usually American media distributed across the globe, the world is not becoming more multicultural but instead is becoming "Americanized."

The Internet has made a huge impact on the spread of information and ideas. Now, people with Internet access can almost instantly gather information on nearly every imaginable subject. A student in the United States can look up Web pages describing a crisis in Africa, while an Asian businessperson might read the financial reports of a competitor half a world away. Never has so much information been so easily available to so many people.

The Internet links societies and peoples across natural and national boundaries. Pictured here is an Internet café in Edfu, Egypt, in 2008.

Economic Globalization

Globalization also manifests itself in economic activity, involving money and finances, as well as trade. Economic globalization can be seen, for example, in agreements such as NAFTA—the North American Free Trade Agreement, between the United States, Canada, and Mexico, which decreases barriers on the flow goods and money across borders. The World Trade Organization (WTO) and its predecessor, the General Agreement on Tariffs and Trades

Many individuals across the world believe the World Bank has too much power over the economies of developing countries. Seen here are protests against the World Bank in Jakarta, Indonesia, in 2004.

(GATT), supervise international trade regulations and work toward fewer restrictions in trade. The WTO is not a part of the United Nations, but the two organizations work closely together in areas of common interest. The UN Conference on Trade and Development (UNCTAD) parallels the WTO in that it too aims to encourage international trade.

Several other global organizations associated with the United Nations are also involved with economic globalization. They include the International Monetary Fund (IMF) and the World Bank. These specialized agencies help arrange the flow of money between countries, setting up loans, for example, from richer countries to poorer ones. They deal with **exchange rates**, and they work with developing countries to end poverty and improve standards of living.

Political Globalization

Political globalization involves an increasing number of international organizations that oversee global policies. Although countries make their own laws and decisions, they are held to certain international standards. For example, almost all the countries in the world are members of the United Nations and have signed the Charter of the United Nations. This means they are responsible for following the principles set out in that charter. They have also accepted the United Nations' Universal Declaration of Human Rights. Although this declaration is not legally binding, it points to common goals for the nations of the world. When countries do commit human rights violations, these acts can be addressed by the United Nations.

Some see political globalization happening as democracy is put forward by the United Nations as the best political system. The goal of the United Nations is that all people have a voice in the directions their nations take. "Democracies are not born overnight, nor built in a year, or by holding one

Labor rights have been an important issue since the late nineteenth century. Pictured here is a demonstration in New York City, in 1914 of the International Workers of the World, one of the most important associations of the early labor movement with members in the United States, Canada, Europe, and Australia.

or two elections," said the UN Secretary-General Ban Ki-moon on the 2012 International Day of Democracy. "They require sustained and painstaking work. Yet, once begun, there can be no going back. Reform must be real. People do not seek authoritarianism with a human face. They want a virtuous circle of rights and opportunity under the rule of law, a vibrant civil society and an enterprising private sector, backed by efficient and accountable state institutions."

Globalization and Labor

Globalization can be seen in the area of labor and employment, as well, with obvious connections to worldwide economic activity. One tie is multinational corporations—huge businesses with offices all over the world, but based most often in developed countries, such as the United States, Great Britain, and Germany. These multinational corporations both sell goods and services around the world and hire employees at their branch offices and factories.

Since labor is generally cheaper in less developed countries, many multinational corporations prefer to operate most of their business in these countries in a practice called "outsourcing." Corporations can increase their profits by hiring foreign workers for less money. Workers in developed countries generally oppose outsourcing, since the practice means fewer, or lower-paying, jobs for local employees.

Globalization and Crime

Globalization has many positive effects—but sometimes it has negative ones as well. Crime is always an issue at the local level, but it can also be a global problem. Quicker means of transportation allow for goods—often illegal drugs—to be carried from country to country. Often drugs are manufactured in countries with fewer regulations and then smuggled into wealthier, industrialized nations.

Smuggling is the main type of global crime, since it involves illegally bringing goods or people across international borders. People-smuggling usually concerns bringing illegal immigrants into a country—those who could not or were not willing to go through the regular legal channels to enter that country. Less often, the practice involves sneaking wanted criminals out of the country in which they have an outstanding arrest warrant. Sometimes people-smuggling includes the additional crime of **forgery** and false identification papers.

The Internet has led to another kind of global crime. Since information from the Internet is available worldwide, people sometimes use it to commit crimes across national borders. Such crimes include fraud and scams of various kinds (for example, trying to raise money for charities that do not exist), identity theft, and the distribution of child pornography. Since not all countries have the same laws, and because of the anonymous nature of the Internet, these

Smuggling illegal drugs across international borders is a crime, especially prevalent as globalization is on the rise. Here, U.S. Immigration and Customs Enforcement officials seize drugs from a tunnel connecting Tijuana, Mexico, and San Diego, California.

criminals can be very difficult to capture and prosecute. Movie, music, and software **piracy** has also become a large problem globally. This happens, for example, when a movie is illegally copied and sold.

* * *

With technology such as the Internet leading to more information on international topics, and with easier transportation, the world is becoming increasingly globalized. Nowadays, the Earth seems like a much smaller place than it did centuries ago. More areas of international life now intersect than ever before. While this is simply a description of the world we live in, globalization can have far-reaching effects—both good and bad. For example, the world's environment is greatly affected by globalization.

When forged money crosses borders, it becomes an international crime. Money is checked for authenticity by using tools like black lights.

CHAPTER ONE

TEXT-DEPENDENT QUESTIONS

1. Define globalization.

2. Name two specific ways globalization can affect a person's life.

3. Name two specific negative consequences of globalization.

RESEARCH PROJECTS

1. Go through your house and complete an inventory of items that are made in different countries. Write a brief report on your observations and conclusions.

2. Look through this chapter and research on the Internet additional photographs to illustrate important points in the text. Write your own captions for each photo.

Shanghai, China, is a beautiful and bustling metropolis, but one plagued by pollution as seen in the smog that hangs over the city.

CHAPTER TWO

Globalization and the Environment

More and more people are becoming concerned about the environment, but environmental degradation has been a problem for thousands of years. People, looking for land where they could plant crops, cleared large amounts of forests. With the trees gone, the soil eroded more easily, blowing away during droughts, falling into the ocean along coastlines, and being carried away by rivers. As people gathered into large cities, air and water pollution became noticeable. Wood smoke and then coal smoke made the air thick and hard to breathe. Garbage and human waste littered the streets and contaminated rivers.

WORDS TO UNDERSTAND

afforestation: conversion of land not previously forested into forest by planting trees.

conservation: preservation, management, and care of natural and cultural resources.

greenhouse gas: gasses such as carbon dioxide and ozone that contribute to the warming of the Earth's atmosphere.

greening: supporting the protection of the environment.

Clouds of polluted smoke from industrial smokestacks blow across international borders. So do billowing sandstorms. Rivers flow from country to country, carrying with them sediments and toxins. No country on Earth can claim that its environmental policies and actions affect only its own citizens.

The world's population has reached seven billion. So many people simply living and using the Earth's resources cannot help but have an effect on the environment. Industrialized nations tend to use more resources and add more pollution to the air and water, but poorer countries contribute as well—for example, through burning large amounts of trees to clear land for farming).

In the past, people took what they needed from the Earth, and often did not worry about **conservation**. The world seemed huge, and many thought they would never run out of land or clean drinking water. If the soil in one place became eroded or stopped growing crops as well, the people could always move somewhere else. There were always some people—or even entire societies—who tried to live in harmony with the Earth, but the issue did not become urgent until recent times. As the world's population increased, and as technological advances demanded

The Dust Bowl was a period of dust storms in the 1930s in midwestern Canada and United States. It was caused by droughts, coupled with poor plowing methods that left the soil incapable of maintaining moisture. Pictured here in 1936 are a farmer and his family in Cimarron County, Oklahoma.

more and more from the Earth, people realized they must learn to care for the Earth to preserve its resources for future generations.

United Nations Environment Programme

When the United Nations was founded in 1945, no specific mention was made of environmental issues, but in the 1960s and 1970s, a new environmental awareness grew among people. The idea that caring for the environment was a global concern grew as well. The Charter of the United Nations stated that the organization wanted "to promote social progress and better standards of life in larger freedom"—and eventually, the United Nations realized that these values needed to include protection of the Earth, since environmental conditions played such a large part in shaping people's lives.

In 1972, the United Nations held the UN Conference on the Human Environment in Stockholm, Sweden. This was the first major international

PROBLEMS OF DEFORESTATION

Roughly 70 percent of the world's animal and plant species live in the world's rainforests, but human activity has a negative impact on those ecosystems. Several decades of clear cutting and farming have devastated the Amazon Rainforest, located in parts of nine South American countries. In Brazil, for example, humans burn more than 6,000 square miles (15,500 square km) of Brazilian jungle a year, roughly the size of Connecticut.

Smoke from the chimneys of power plants, like this one in Finland, can travel hundreds of miles and across borders.

Since the founding the UN Environmental Programme in 1972, the environmental movement has become more and more globalized. Pictured here is a rally in 2013 in Madrid, Spain, organized to support Russian activists who were detained for protesting against drilling in the Arctic.

meeting at which global environmental issues were discussed and the role of the international community was recognized. Because of the Stockholm Conference, the United Nations founded the United Nations Environment Programme (UNEP).

The stated purpose of UNEP is "to provide leadership and encourage partnership in caring for the environment by inspiring, informing, and enabling nations and peoples to improve their quality of life without compromising that of future generations."

A major document created at the Stockholm Conference was the Declaration on the United Nations Conference on the Human Environment, often called the Stockholm Declaration. The Stockholm Declaration lists seven proclamations and twenty-six principles that guide the actions of the United Nations on environmental issues. These principles cover issues such as economic and social development, as well as strictly environmental concerns. For example, Principle 10 states:

FROM THE "STOCKHOLM DECLARATION"
PARAGRAPH 6

A point has been reached in history when we must shape our actions throughout the world with a more prudent care for their environmental consequences. Through ignorance or indifference we can do massive and irreversible harm to the earthly environment on which our life and well-being depend. Conversely, through fuller knowledge and wiser action, we can achieve for ourselves and our posterity a better life in an environment more in keeping with human needs and hopes. There are broad vistas for the enhancement of environmental quality and the creation of a good life. What is needed is an enthusiastic but calm state of mind and intense but orderly work. For the purpose of attaining freedom in the world of nature, man must use knowledge to build, in collaboration with nature, a better environment. To defend and improve the human environment for present and future generations has become an imperative goal for mankind—a goal to be pursued together with, and in harmony with, the established and fundamental goals of peace and of worldwide economic and social development.

Source: World Service Authority (http://www.worldservice.org/stockholm.html)

Overuse of freshwater in places such as the American Southwest has increased the likelihood of drought and desertification. Pictured here is dry and caked mud in Gabbs, Nevada, an area close to Las Vegas, one of most rapidly expanding urban areas in the Great Basin Desert of the western United States.

Kids enjoy the sights and sounds—including this porcupine—at the celebration of the International Day for Biological Diversity on May 22, 2011, in Malaga, Spain. World Biodiversity Day, as it's also called, was established by the UN General Assembly in 1993.

For the developing countries, stability of prices and adequate earnings for primary commodities and raw materials are essential to environmental management, since economic factors as well as ecological processes must be taken into account.

Since its creation in 1972, UNEP has grown into a major part of the United Nations. The organization monitors sixteen different environmental issues, ranging from freshwater access to climate change to sports and the environment. Eight divisions also operate within UNEP, dealing with topics like environmental policy and public information.

Rio Earth Summit

In 1992, the United Nations Conference on Environment and Development (UNCED)—better known as the Earth Summit—was held in Rio de Janeiro, Brazil. Held twenty years after the Stockholm Convention, the Earth Summit was a massive conference, with representatives from 172 countries attending, over a hundred of them heads of state. For the first time, the majority of the world's governments acknowledged the need for real change in environmental policy in order to protect the Earth for future generations.

Five major documents came out of the Rio Earth Summit, including:

- the Rio Declaration on Environment and Development
- Agenda 21
- the Convention on Biological Diversity
- the Statement of Forest Principles
- the Framework Convention on Climate Change.

The Rio Declaration built on the Stockholm Declaration, listing twenty-seven principles "working towards international agreements which respect the interests of all and protect the integrity of the global environmental and developmental system." In 2012, a third summit, Rio+20, was held. During that conference, countries renewed their commitment to sustainability. Those who attended called for a wide range of actions on such issues as making the UN Environment Programme stronger. Whereas the Rio Declaration listed general principles such as "Human beings are at the centre of concerns for sustainable development. They are entitled to a healthy and productive life in harmony with nature," Agenda 21 was more detailed. Agenda 21 listed specific issues, like "Combating Poverty" and "Protection of the Atmosphere," then listed a series of goals for each issue together with actions to be taken by governments to improve problem areas.

The issue of deforestation was of particular concern at the Earth Summit. This interest led to the Statement of Forest Principles, a document

IMPACT OF CLIMATE CHANGE

As climate change progresses, its impact is threatening food production and causing sea levels to rise, among other things. UNEP helps countries adapt to climate change and aids them in reducing their carbon footprint. The United Nations now holds regular summits on the issue. For example, those attending the 2014 United Nations Climate Summit in New York City announced plans to combat the worst effects of climate change by finalizing a new universal agreement in 2015.

The effects of deforestation like this in Palawan in the Philippines is wide-ranging. They include the loss of biodiversity as well as the increased potential for erosion due to clearing the land of trees that hold the soil in place.

devoted entirely to the supervision and protection of the world's forests. "Efforts should be undertaken towards the **greening** of the world," the document stated. "All countries, notably developed countries, should take positive and transparent action towards reforestation, **afforestation** and forest conservation, as appropriate."

The Rio Declaration, Agenda 21, and the Statement of Forest Principles were not legally binding on the international community. Two other documents were produced at the Earth Summit, though, that were legally binding. These international treaties (called conventions) were the United Nations Convention on Biological Diversity and the United Nations Framework Convention on Climate Change.

Biological diversity, or biodiversity, refers to the variety of plants and animals living on Earth. The purpose of the Convention on Biological Diversity was to protect this vast array of life.

The main goal of the Framework Convention on Climate Change was to reduce **greenhouse gas** emissions that could lead to global warming.

The original convention did not set the emission limits, but allowed for later additions, or protocols. In 1997, a meeting in Japan produced the Kyoto Protocol, which set the limits on greenhouse gas production. The Kyoto Protocol required that, between 2008 and 2012, countries reduce their 1990 levels of emissions by 5.2 percent. In 2013, the Doha amendment to the protocol went into effect that extended the time period by another eight years, while urging countries to reduce emissions even further by 2020. While most people across the world now believe that climate change is a real phenomenon linked to the burning of fossil fuels, the Kyoto Protocol is still controversial to some, especially industry owners, since these reductions would require major expenses and changes in their businesses.

United Nations Division for Sustainable Development

At the Rio Earth Summit in 1992, the United Nations founded the Commission on Sustainable Development. The job of the commission is to monitor the progress of the actions set out in Agenda 21.

The commission is led by the United Nations Division for Sustainable Development (UNDSD), itself a part of the UN Economic and Social Development Council. The mission of the UNDSD is "development that meets the needs of the present without compromising the ability of future generations to meet their own needs." The UNDSD works closely with the UNEP, since their interests overlap to such a great extent.

* * *

The UN's mission extended naturally into caring for the Earth and its natural resources. The United Nations strongly believes that we must look after the Earth's resources so they will be around for people to enjoy in the future. The UN's concern about the environment shows itself in the organization's contribution to taking care of the health needs of the world's people.

CHAPTER TWO

TEXT-DEPENDENT QUESTIONS

1. When was the first United Nations Conference on the Human Environment held?

2. Summarize the Stockholm Declaration.

3. What did the Kyoto Protocol set out to do? What were the results?

RESEARCH PROJECTS

1. Research and create a map of areas around the world that are in danger of deforestation.

2. Research one major environmental problem facing some part of the world today. Write a short essay discussing whether globalization has improved the problem or made it worse.

A medieval illustration of the Black Death, the plague that killed nearly one-third of Europe's population.

CHAPTER THREE

Globalization and Health

Diseases have never recognized international borders. They can be carried through air and water, passed on from person to person, or spread by the bites of infected animals. The United Nations is concerned with all areas of global health issues. These concerns include both stopping the spread of infectious diseases and making sure that people have better access to health care and the tools they need to live healthy lives.

 WORDS TO UNDERSTAND

attainment: achievement of a goal.

influenza: a highly contagious disease that manifests itself in fever, aches, sore throat, and cold symptoms.

smallpox: highly contagious disease caused by a virus and marked by high fever and formation of scar-producing pustules.

ultrasound: a technique using high-frequency sound waves reflecting off internal body parts to produce medical images.

Global Epidemics

History tells the stories of dozens of plagues and outbreaks of disease. For centuries, these epidemics were restrained by the limits of travel. Sometimes, a disease was so deadly it killed people too quickly to spread very far; people who caught the disease died before they could travel and spread it.

More often, the type of travel available at the time limited the epidemic. For example, the Black Death spread across Europe in the fourteenth century, killing nearly a third of the population. Merchants and other travelers moving on foot, on horseback, or by boat carried the disease around the continent. In the twentieth century, soldiers returning home after World War I spread a deadly form of **influenza** around the world. Since travel was so much quicker and easier in the 1900s than it was in the 1300s, the disease was able to affect millions more people than it would have centuries earlier.

Bacteria and viruses are not the only cause of global epidemics, though. Many argue that the influence of Western culture has created an epidemic of obesity and heart disease. People in industrialized nations tend to eat diets high in fats and sugars, which bring about a whole set of health problems.

In developing nations, on the other hand, the health epidemics are more often due to poverty and lack of adequate medical care. For example, in Africa and Asia, HIV/AIDS has struck millions of people. Health-care workers struggle to help educate people on how to prevent the disease, as well as to treat those already infected. In 2015, some 35 million people around the world were living with HIV/AIDS, including more than 3.2 million children under the age of fifteen. Moreover, in 2013, about 2.1 million became infected with HIV. In Sub-Sahara Africa, 25 million people were living with HIV in 2012.

THE NEED FOR IMMUNIZATION

Immunization prevents nearly 3 million deaths each year, but 20 percent of the world's children are not vaccinated against such life-threatening diseases such as influenza and meningitis. In 2013, some 21.8 million newborns did not receive any type of vaccine.

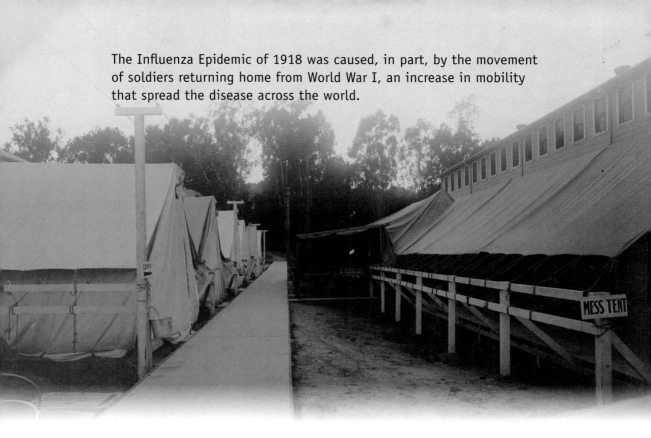

The Influenza Epidemic of 1918 was caused, in part, by the movement of soldiers returning home from World War I, an increase in mobility that spread the disease across the world.

In 2014, the virus Ebola emerged as a major threat in West Africa. The United Nations along with other organizations and nations converged on the region to help stop the spread of the deadly disease. The World Health Organization was charged with the overall health strategy, while other UN agencies brought their expertise under direction of the UN emergency health mission tasked with coordinating the effort. The United Nations Children's Fund shipped 3,000 metric tons of supplies to help fight the spread of Ebola in West Africa.

Another "epidemic" faced by very poor countries is maternal mortality—the death of women in childbirth. In 2005, the chances of women dying in childbirth in parts of Africa were one thousand times greater than in developed countries. As of 2013, 99 percent of material mortality occurred in the developing world. And while the material mortality rate—the number of women who die in childbirth compared to the number giving birth—has dropped by 2.6 percent between 1990 and 2013, that number is less than half the drop envisioned in the Millennium Development Goals.

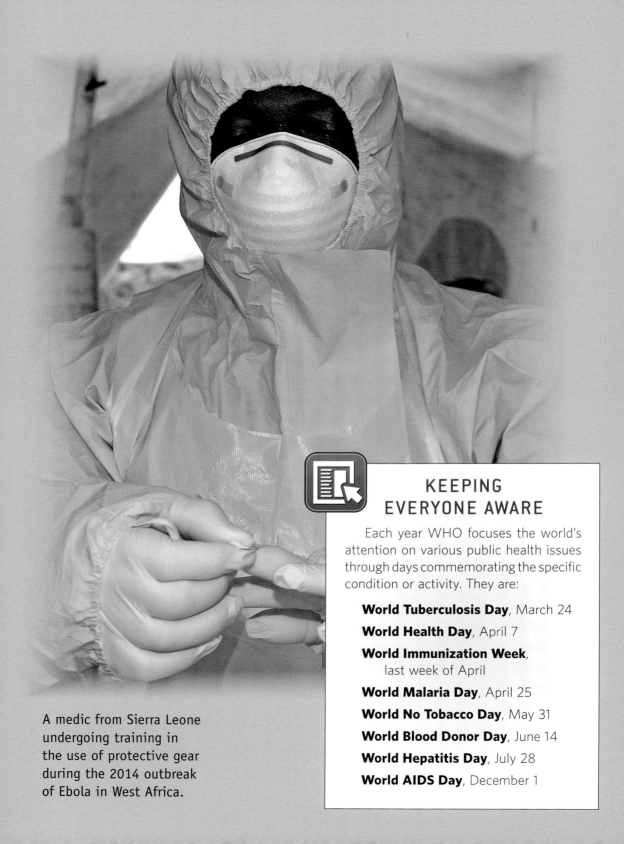

A medic from Sierra Leone undergoing training in the use of protective gear during the 2014 outbreak of Ebola in West Africa.

KEEPING EVERYONE AWARE

Each year WHO focuses the world's attention on various public health issues through days commemorating the specific condition or activity. They are:

World Tuberculosis Day, March 24

World Health Day, April 7

World Immunization Week, last week of April

World Malaria Day, April 25

World No Tobacco Day, May 31

World Blood Donor Day, June 14

World Hepatitis Day, July 28

World AIDS Day, December 1

The World Health Organization headquarters in Geneva, Switzerland.

The World Health Organization

The World Health Organization (WHO) is a part of the United Nations and focuses on health concerns of all kinds. Its stated goal is "the **attainment** of all peoples of the highest possible level of health." Many medical officers and scientists work for WHO, overseeing hundreds of different health issues, from **smallpox** to depression. These health issues also include positive steps toward better health, such as nutrition and diagnostic techniques and procedures—for example, X-rays and **ultrasounds**.

Due to the overlapping nature of the UN's structure, the work of WHO often intersects with the work of its other agencies. For example, at least a dozen UN bodies, including WHO, are involved in helping the Asian people after the tsunami of December 2004. And in November 2013, when Tropical Storm Haiyan hit the Philippines, the UN's International Telecommunications Union, donated satellite terminals, phones, and laptop computers to help WHO workers establish communications and to help Filipinos communicate with each other. Many agencies also come together to assist during famines. In emergency situations, the agencies work closely with the United Nations Office for the Coordination of

Humanitarian Affairs (OCHA). The agencies deal with different aspects of the disaster or emergency situation, with WHO taking care of the health concerns, and, for example, UNICEF focusing on the children involved in the crisis, while the United Nations World Food Programme (WFP) brings in supplies to feed the hungry.

For WHO, globalization is a mixed blessing. As the world becomes more connected, the nature of threats changes. Diseases spread extremely quickly among industrialized nations, because of the frequent travel between countries. This makes serious outbreaks more difficult to control and isolate and means that doctors must work more quickly to stop the spread of the disease. On the other hand, globalization has increased the flow of medical supplies across borders. WHO has the organizational structure to be able to quickly send teams of medical personnel to sites of disease outbreak or health crises like famines or natural disasters.

As WHO takes on scores of health issues across the globe, it continually comes face to face with one overwhelming issue—poverty. Not only a problem in itself, poverty contributes to many of the world's health issues.

The Beagle Brigade, part of the inspection service of the U.S. Department of Agriculture, searches for contaminated food in luggage at airports.

CHAPTER THREE

TEXT-DEPENDENT QUESTIONS

1. In what century did the Black Death spread across Europe?

2. What disease did soldiers returning home from World War I spread?

3. Which virus threatened West Africa in 2014?

RESEARCH PROJECTS

1. Make a list of the major diseases the World Health Organization is working to eradicate.

2. Break into small groups and create a public awareness advertisement for a disease the World Health Organization is combating. The advertisement can take the form of a simple newspaper or television ad, or a multi-media presentation using any electronic platform you wish to use.

Poverty is a global problem and reaches communities
like this hillside slum in Lima, Peru.

CHAPTER FOUR

Globalization and Poverty

In the world today, 2.4 billion people live on the equivalent of less than two dollars a day. Most do not have access to clean drinking water. Extreme poverty—when people cannot afford to buy basic necessities such as food—affects populations throughout the world, not just in the poorest countries, but also in the richest countries as well.

Poverty is complex, affected by and influencing many other issues. For instance, poor people are less likely to get adequate health care and therefore often suffer from diseases and conditions not usually seen in developed countries. Those in poverty also are more likely to live in environments that are not protected and therefore more damaging to human health.

WORDS TO UNDERSTAND

collateral: related to; occurring at the same time.

destitution: extreme poverty.

disparities: differences between groups or things.

eradication: the process of doing away with.

literacy: the ability to read and write.

reiterate: to repeat something.

International trade is another factor affecting the lives of poor people. While occasionally helpful in increasing economic growth in developing countries, it often presents difficulties. Countries with workforces that are not highly skilled or educated compared to others find it hard to compete in the international market with products other than natural resources. But the mining of metals, such as copper, important in a range of applications, and rare earth elements important in electronic devices, which are being extracted in countries such as China, Vietnam, Malawi, and Tanzania, can be dangerous both to laborers and as well as the environment.

One way out of extraction-based economic growth is improving education. And indeed people living in poverty usually have limited access to education. Sometimes they are not able to go to school at all, while other times their schooling is inadequate. Without education, and especially without being able to read or write, a person is generally not able to rise out of poverty and improve life circumstances.

The Nchanga Copper Mine in Zambia, in southern Africa, in 2008.

EDUCATION FOR ALL?

Statistics about education convey **disparities** among men, women, and youth. In 2012, the global adult **literacy** rate, for those fifteen years and older, stood at 80 percent for women and 89 percent men in 2012. At that same time, 92 percent of male youths were literate, and only 60 percent of all countries had youth literacy rates of 95 percent or higher.

Programs like USAID's Empowerment through Literacy Education Access Project have helped people like this Maasai woman in northern Tanzania learn Swahili, which gives them greater opportunities to learn other skills.

The number of people living in extreme poverty over the last century has not changed as much as the gap between the incomes of the rich and the poor people of the world. According to the 2014 Human Development Report of the UNDP, almost 1.5 billion people in 91 developing countries live in poverty. Although poverty has been on the decline, almost 800 million people were at risk of slipping back into poverty. But at the top of the income scale, in 2013, eight percent of the world's population earned half of the world's total income. This disparity is a primary concern to many policy makers as they attempt to solve issues relating to poverty.

The United Nations Development Programme

Although most United Nations agencies deal with poverty in some way, the UNDP is the most directly concerned with the issue. UNDP's Web site states that it is "an organization advocating for change and connecting countries to knowledge, experience and resources to help people build a better life."

POOREST NATIONS IN THE WORLD

Among the twenty poorest nations in the world in 2014, eighteen were in Africa. That number is not surprising considering that the continent is wracked by drought, famine, lack of clean water, and poor health care, as well as war and civil conflict. Haiti is the world's poorest nation outside of Africa.

Helping people build better lives is also a very central part of the Charter of the United Nations and the Universal Declaration of Human Rights. The UNDP works to make this a reality by dealing with poverty reduction, specifically in the context of sustainable development, that is, economic growth achieved in an enduring way, without **collateral** damage to the environment.

United Nations Decades for the Eradication of Poverty

The United Nations is very concerned with ending poverty and helping people live better, more fulfilling lives In 2010, Secretary-General Ban Ki-moon told students at the UNA-USA Model United Nations Conference that it is essential that people be lifted up from desperate economic situations. "I believe in a world of justice and human rights for all. A world where girls can grow up free of fear of abuse. A world where women are treated with the respect and dignity that is their right. A world where poverty is not acceptable. My dear young friends, you can make this your world."

In December 1995, the General Assembly of the United Nations named the years between 1997 and 2006 as the United Nations Decade for the **Eradication** of Poverty. The theme of the decade was "eradicating poverty is an ethical, social, political and economic imperative of humankind." To accomplish this mission, the United Nations promised to work with those

The International Fund for Agricultural Development is one of the specialized UN agencies involved in poverty reduction; it helps indigenous people maintain their traditional livelihoods while ensuring environmental protection. Pictured here is a woman tending sheep in the Mongolian grasslands of northern China, around the locality of Taipusi.

living in poverty to help improve their way of life, not to simply give them handouts of food or other goods. One expert, reporting to the United Nations Commission on Human Rights (later the Human Rights Council), said:

> It is essential to set in motion machinery for participation which involves the poorest at every stage of the policies devised to help them. Only thus can concrete and lasting results be achieved. Only as they rediscover their full range of rights and freedoms shall we see emerging in all their splendor the human beings behind the poverty-scarred faces.

The battle against poverty continued after the decade was up. In 2008, the UN began its Second United Nations Decade for the Eradication of Poverty. At the time, the UN **reiterated** its stance that poverty was the "greatest global challenge" facing the planet. The theme of the Second United Nations Decade for the Eradication of Poverty was codified in General Assembly Resolution 63/230. The resolution set "full employment and decent work for all," as the decade's goal. The resolution called for a more integrated UN response to meet this challenge.

International Day for the Eradication of Poverty

Beginning in 1993, the General Assembly of the United Nations decided to hold an annual International Day for the Eradication of Poverty. Every year on October 17, the nations of the world pay tribute to those living in extreme poverty. This yearly emphasis serves as a reminder of the large goal the United Nations and the people of the world want to achieve—the goal of completely ridding the world of poverty.

The ceremonies on this day usually include stories, essays, and songs by young people, as well as speeches and a panel discussion on some aspect of poverty. The goal of the International Day for the Eradication of Poverty is a greater awareness of the misery poverty causes, how it steals from people their basic freedoms and human rights, and how it must not be tolerated.

Poverty is not only a problem in developing countries. In fact, homelessness is a pressing issue in many communities in the United States and other wealthy countries.

Progress Toward Ending Poverty

Since poverty is such a complex issue, with many causes and affected by many issues, bringing all out of poverty and helping them live better lives are difficult goals to achieve. One step toward ending poverty is giving everyone the chance to go to school, at least at the primary level, so they can learn to read and write, can learn simple math skills, and can learn something about the world. These skills give people a huge boost toward being able to make something better out of their own lives. Education is not always enough to overcome poverty, of course, but without basic educational skills, leaving poverty behind becomes almost impossible.

In 2000, all the UN Member States committed to eight Millennium Development Goals, which were to be met by 2015. Many of them related to poverty, either directly or indirectly; for example, the first goal was:

"Eradicate extreme poverty and hunger" and halving the proportion of people who live in extreme poverty—defined as living on less than $1.25 per day—was met five years ahead of the 2015 target date. While this translated into 700 million fewer individuals living in extreme poverty, there remain 1.2 billion living in such conditions. Indeed, the UN's 2015 development agenda maintains a laser sharp focus on poverty reduction and renews its commitment by adding the dimension of sustainability to its policies and programs.

At the 2014 International Day for the Eradication of Poverty, UN Secretary-General Ban Ki-moon said:

Entrenched poverty and prejudice, and vast gulfs between wealth and **destitution**, can undermine the fabric of societies and lead to instability. Where poverty holds sway, people are held back. Lives disfigured by poverty are cruel, mean and, often, short. As we prepare the post-2015 sustainable development agenda and address the threat of climate change, we must not lose sight of our most fundamental obligation: to eliminate poverty in all its forms. We must also end the marginalization of people living in poverty. Their knowledge and perspectives are vital if we are to find meaningful, durable solutions. I urge Member States and all partners to act decisively together to eradicate poverty and build a sustainable, peaceful, prosperous and equitable future for all. Our aim must be prosperity for all, not just a few.

Poverty is such pervasive problem that it can get lost in statistics, sometimes forgetting that behind those staggeringly huge numbers are real people. Poverty destroys people's basic human rights and freedoms, taking away their ability to choose the directions their lives will take. Freedom to choose one's religion is one right people have struggled with for thousands of years, in industrialized nations as well as in developing ones.

A poor community in Cambodia, one of the poorest countries in Southeast Asia—with 18.6 percent of the population living on less than $1.25 per day.

CHAPTER FOUR

TEXT-DEPENDENT QUESTIONS

1. What is the world literacy rate for male youths?

2. When did the Second United Nations Decade for the Eradication of Poverty begin?

3. What is one of the new focuses of the UN's post-2015 development agenda?

RESEARCH PROJECTS

1. Research and create a bar chart showing the literacy rate in three developing countries and three developing countries. What can you conclude?

2. Research some of the groups and organizations in your community that help people in poverty. Create a list describing what each group does.

Buddhism is a popular religion in countries like China and others in eastern Asia. This statue of the Buddha is located in Da Lat, Vietnam.

CHAPTER FIVE

Globalization and Religion

The world is filled with many religions. Many of these religions have welcomed the process of globalization, taking advantage of a more connected world to spread their beliefs to other people. On the other hand, as the world has become increasingly globalized, some religious groups worry that the spread of cultural ideas and values might be harmful to their beliefs. They worry about cultural differences being swept away and wonder if soon all diversity will be gone. They speculate that the people of the world will all start to act and think in the same ways and fear that the distinctiveness of their own religion might be lost.

WORDS TO UNDERSTAND

advocate: a person who acts and speaks on behalf of an issue.

extremists: those who have radical political or religious beliefs.

livelihood: way of supporting oneself.

nationalistic: showing extreme devotion to one nation and its interests above all others.

rapporteur: an official researcher whose role it is to report regularly to an organization.

These fears sometimes lead people to become very **nationalistic**, promoting their own culture and nation over global concerns. While there is nothing wrong with patriotism on its own, some **extremists** react violently and launch attacks against other countries and peoples. In 2014, UN Secretary-General Ban Ki-moon opened the General Assembly's annual session by criticizing extremists that have caused widespread devastation in many countries, including Syria, Iraq, and Ukraine. "It has been a terrible year for the principles of the United Nations Charter," he said. "From barrel bombs to beheadings, from the deliberate starvation of civilians to the assault on hospitals, U.N. shelters and aid convoys, human rights and the rule of law are under attack."

The main prayer hall of the Umayyid Mosque in Damascus, Syria, in 2004. In 2013, the mosque was severely damaged in the Syrian Civil War.

RELIGIOUS DIVERSITY

The most diverse religious country, based on population, is the small-island nation of Singapore, located on the southern tip of Malaysia. Eighteen percent of Singapore's 5 million people identify as Christian; 14 percent Muslim; 16 percent have no religious affiliation; 5 percent Hindu, and 34 percent Buddhist. Ten percent practice other religions, and the balance is made up those who practice folk or traditional religions. One of the least diverse religious countries is Iran, in which more than 99 percent of its population is Muslim.

The Millennium World Peace Summit of Religious and Spiritual Leaders

In August of 2000, two thousand religious leaders from all over the world came together at the United Nations headquarters in New York City to discuss how the religions of the world could make an impact on world peace. Although the Millennium World Peace Summit of Religious and Spiritual Leaders was not an official UN-sponsored conference, it was associated with the United Nations, and the secretary-general spoke at the gathering. The summit was organized largely by Bawa Jain, an advocate of interfaith dialogues, and funded by billionaire Ted Turner and the United Nations Foundation, an organization he founded dedicated to assisting the work of the United Nations. The organizers of the summit hoped that by bringing together representatives from over fifteen major faiths, world religious leaders could begin to talk about ways to end religious fighting and help bring peace to the world.

At the opening of the convention, Bawa Jain, secretary-general of the summit, listed a number of goals he hoped the gathering would accomplish. He asked all delegates to sign a Commitment to Global Peace, and he proposed creating a council of religious leaders to work with the United Nations. From the United Nations, Jain asked for three things: for another World Peace Summit of Religious and Spiritual Leaders to be held every ten years, the creation of an Office of Religious Affairs at the United Nations, and partnership with a Council of Religious and Spiritual Leaders.

Representatives of many of the world religions were represented at the Millennium World Peace Summit, including Jainism, one of the oldest of the world's religions. Pictured here is a Jain temple in Calcutta, India.

The delegates who attended the summit were frustrated that the meetings mainly consisted of discussing general ideas instead of specific plans of action. Some felt no real progress was made toward solving actual problems. Despite this, the summit produced several clear results. The Web site of the World Council of Religious Leaders—itself formed as a product of the Millennium World Peace Summit in 2002—lists seven outcomes of the summit:

- the signing of the Commitment to Global Peace
- initiation of a process to form a World Council of Religious and Spiritual Leaders
- cofounding of the Religious Leaders Initiative of the World Economic Forum
- a partnership with the United Nations' High Commission for Human Rights
- establishment of a Global Commission for the Preservation of Sacred Sites
- the opening of international interfaith dialogue
- the Congress on the Preservation of Religious Diversity.

The World Council of Religious and Spiritual Leaders has followed up with several activities as an outgrowth of the first summit. One such outcome is the joining of Jewish and Hindu leaders in February 2007, during which they confirmed their desire to maintain the traditions of their own faiths, while respecting the rights of other faith communities, and affirmed the importance of social responsibility within their own societies as well as the world in general and the need to address the concerns of poverty and inequality together.

The Commitment to Global Peace condemned "all violence perpetrated in the name of religion" and acknowledged "the value of religious and ethnic diversity." Hundreds of the delegates signed the nonbinding statement at the Summit, and afterward the document continued to circulate throughout the world, collecting the signatures of religious and spiritual leaders. Among its objectives, the Commitment to Global Peace included, "To lead humanity by word and deed in a renewed commitment to ethical and spiritual values, which include a deep sense of respect for all life and for each person's inherent dignity and right to live in a world free of violence."

One aspect of the Millennium World Peace Summit not accepted by all delegates or religious groups was the statement by several leaders, including Bawa Jain, that all religions are equal. Jain stated that he believes people of all religions get their insights from the same source and that the outward appearance of religions is not important. Although some delegates approved of this idea, others, including the delegation representing the Roman Catholic Church, objected. While most agreed that religious leaders should work together to help the cause of world peace, many denied that to do so they must declare all religions equal.

Many people in Japan practice Shintoism, which focuses on the spiritual powers in the natural world. This picture shows the random fortunes placed by people at the Kasuga Taisha Shrine in Nara, Japan.

SNAPSHOT OF THE WORLD'S RELIGIONS

In 2012, according to a study by the Pew Research Center, 80 percent of the people in the world identified with a particular religious group. The study of more than 230 countries and territories estimated that out of 7 billion people on the planet, 5.8 billion have some religious affiliation. Most, 2.2 billion, identified as Christians; 1.6 billion identified as Muslim; 1 billion identified as Hindu; 500 million Buddhists, and 14 million Jews. The percentages for each religion are as follows:

Christian: 31.5 percent

Muslim: 23.2 percent

Unaffiliated: 16.3 percent

Hindu: 15 percent

Buddhist: 7.1 percent

Folk Religions: 5.9 (including traditional African, Chinese, Native American, and Australian aboriginal religions)

Jewish: 0.20 percent

Other religions: 0.8 (including Bahai, Sikhs, Taoists, and other faiths)

In Jerusalem, the Temple Mount is the site of worship for three religions—Judaism, Islam, and Christianity. Pictured here are the Western Wall, where Jews gather to pray, and the Dome of the Rock, which is frequently the source of clashes between Jews and Muslims, whose access to the Dome of the Rock is contested by many Orthodox rabbis.

The United Nations and Religion

Traditionally, the United Nations has avoided the topic of religion. Toward the end of the twentieth century, though, the United Nations became more associated with interfaith dialogues, such as the Millennium Summit discussed above, hoping to use the power of religion and religious beliefs in people's lives to help further the goals of the United Nations.

One way the United Nations has always been concerned with religion, however, is in the area of human rights. The Universal Declaration of Human Rights, adopted in 1948, states:

> Everyone has the right to freedom of thought, conscience and religion; this right includes freedom to change his religion or belief, and freedom, either alone or in community with others and in public or private, to manifest his religion or belief in teaching, practice, worship and observance.

In 1946, the United Nations created the Commission on Human Rights. The commission's job was to oversee all areas of human rights. In 1986, the commission appointed

Heiner Bielefeld, the UN's special rapporteur on freedom of religion or belief (at left), talking to Jeremy Gunn, a professor at the Al Akhawayn University in Morocco, at the World Humanist Congress in 2011 in Oslo, Norway.

a special **rapporteur** for freedom of religion or belief. The special rapporteur is an individual whose job is to monitor religious freedom and "to examine incidents and governmental actions in all parts of the world which were inconsistent with the provisions of the Declaration on the Elimination of All Forms of Intolerance and of Discrimination Based on Religion or Belief, and to recommend remedial measures for such situations." The special rapporteur then reports to the Commission on Human Rights and to the General Assembly of the United Nations.

Buddhist monks dedicate their lives to meditative living. Depending on the country, a monk may wear a yellow, red, or orange robe.

Indigenous Rights

Indigenous peoples—whose ancestors originally inhabited a territory—have unique cultures, living as minorities in the midst of other, dominant cultures. They include Native American populations and Aboriginal groups living in Australia and New Zealand. But native groups whose cultures and **livelihoods** are threatened can be found in many other countries throughout the world.

In 2000, the United Nations created a Permanent Forum on Indigenous Issues to advise the Economic and Social Council of the United Nations on native peoples' issues and how best to address them. Part of this task includes preserving indigenous cultures, including native religions. The United Nations went a step further when the Commission on Human Rights (later the Human Rights Council) established a special rapporteur position to investigate and report on the rights of indigenous groups in 2001. The mandate for the rapporteur was renewed in 2004 and in 2007. Indigenous religions were also included in the 2000 Millennium World Peace Summit of Religious and Spiritual Leaders.

COMBATING RELIGIOUS INTOLERANCE

In the spring of 2015, the U.N. Office of the High Commissioner for Human Rights hosted a forum in London to combat religious intolerance. "Intolerance and discrimination, especially if based on religion and belief, represent a serious threat to the peacefulness and stability of societies," Hanif al-Qassim, the chairman of the Geneva Centre for Human Rights Advancement and Global Dialogue, told reporters before the gathering. "It is therefore our duty to raise awareness on good practices and challenges ahead, and to enhance governments' capacities to combat religious-based discrimination through concrete measures and agreed follow-up mechanisms."

The process of globalization has affected religion simply because religious groups now have greater contact with each other. And the United Nations is concerned that globalizing forces not lessen people's freedom of religion. The UN, dealing with globalization on many levels, often finds it must make a determined effort to maximize the positive aspects of globalization while minimizing the negative aspects.

Intolerance and persecution of religious minorities, such as Muslim Uyghur communities living in China, have been addressed by the UN in a range of ways, including the Universal Declaration of Human Rights. Shown here are two Uyghur girls in Xinjiang, China.

CHAPTER FIVE

TEXT-DEPENDENT QUESTIONS

1. Why do some religious groups fear globalization?

2. What is the difference between a nationalist and an extremist?

3. Explain the concept of freedom of religion.

RESEARCH PROJECTS

1. Research a world religion and describe in a computer-slide show or in an oral report how globalization has affected that religion.

2. Take a survey of the religious affiliation of your classmates and create a bar chart showing the numbers.

Flags in front of the UN headquarters in New York City. Many nations work together within the United Nations—a potent symbol of one of the most promising aspects of globalization.

CHAPTER SIX

Globalization and the United Nations

The United Nations is a massive global organization, with many divisions and sub-organizations dealing with dozens of world issues. Since it is so involved with international affairs, much of what the organization does affects cultural globalization. The job of the United Nations is to work with the countries of the world to bring about peaceful resolutions to conflicts and to help people live better lives. As countries communicate with each other more and work together with greater understanding, the process of globalization unavoidably speeds up.

 WORDS TO UNDERSTAND

bureaucracy: a complex system of administration, usually referring to a government or corporation.

liability: legal responsibility for an action.

sovereignty: self-rule.

standardize: remove variations and irregularities and make all types or examples of something the same or bring them into conformity with each other.

One effect of such globalization has been the need for increased international regulations. Although all countries have different laws, frequent international connections have led to the development of international law governing these interactions.

International Law

In general, international law can mean one of two things: laws dealing with nations and the conflicts between them, or the laws affecting the legal disputes between two private citizens from different countries. The second of these two is private international law, which does not always have set laws governing legal interactions. Generally, the people involved in the lawsuit must choose which country's courts will hear the case. The Hague Conference on Private International Law has worked for over a century to **standardize** laws affecting private citizens.

The Hague Conference is not an organization of the United Nations, but often works closely with the United Nations to create guiding legal policies. Some major Hague agreements (called conventions) have included declarations on international child abductions and determining which country's laws take precedence in situations such as product **liability** and traffic accidents between people of different nationalities.

As a global organization, the United Nations is much more involved with the laws dealing with relationships between countries than with those dealing with individuals. In 1947, the United Nations formed the International Law Commission to look into legal questions and put together recommendations about what is needed to be made into law.

International Court of Justice

One of the principle bodies of the United Nations is the International Court of Justice (ICJ)—often called the World Court—based in The Hague in the Netherlands. The ICJ has two main tasks: to resolve legal disputes between nations and to give opinions on legal questions asked by international

One of the first implementations of international law following the establishment of the United Nations was the World War II war crimes trials. Pictured here is Hideki Tojo, Japan's premier and war minister, who stands listening to his death sentence delivered in 1948.

agencies. The results of the first are legally binding, while the opinions given are not legally binding. Many international treaties include clauses stating that the ICJ will decide any disagreements that occur due to the treaty. However, the ICJ has no power to make sure its verdicts are carried out and must, like most courts, rely on other organizations to uphold its rulings. The General Assembly or the Security Council of the United Nations has the power to take actions against countries if it chooses, for example, by imposing economic sanctions against them.

One of the weaknesses of the ICJ, though, is that at times, one party will refuse to abide by the verdict. If, for example, the refusing party is one of the five permanent members of the Security Council—and therefore can veto any decision—nothing can be done. This was the case in 1984 when the ICJ ruled that the United States had used unlawful force against the government of Nicaragua. The court ordered the United States to pay reparations to Nicaragua, but America refused.

Since its creation in 1946, the ICJ has made rulings on ninety cases and given twenty-five advisory opinions. As of 2015, the court had no open cases and thirteen pending cases. These cases include border disputes, questions of **sovereignty**, and nuclear disarmament.

International Criminal Court

In 2002, the United Nations established the International Criminal Court (ICC) to try people accused of genocide, war crimes, and crimes against humanity. The ICJ took care of judging the responsibility of nations, but had no authority over the individuals accused of such serious crimes.

Although established by the United Nations through the Rome Statute, the ICC now functions as an independent organization. The court works

The Peace Palace in The Hague is home to the International Court of Justice.

ICC CASE FILE #1

In 2012, Thomas Lubanga Dyilo, founder and leader of the Union of Congolese Patriots (UPC), became the first person ever convicted by the ICC. Dyilo was found guilty of war crimes for "enlisting and conscripting children under the age of fifteen and using them to participate actively in hostilities" in the Democratic Republic of the Congo. He was sentenced to fourteen years in prison. At the time, the UPC was one of the main groups that participated in a civil war between the Hema and Lendu ethnic groups.

closely with the United Nations, but is not directly governed by it. Not all the 193 UN member nations have chosen to ratify the ICC statute. As of 2014, 122 countries had ratified or acceded the statute. Countries refusing to accept the ICC include the United States, China, and Israel. The United States claims it will not be held accountable to the ICC because it fears other countries that dislike the United States will bring "frivolous or politically motivated prosecutions" against it.

Either a country or the UN Security Council must refer the cases on which the court rules. As of the beginning of 2015, the ICC had received complaints about alleged illegal actions in 139 countries. The prosecutor of the ICC had opened investigations into nine of these situations.

The Global Compact

While international organizations such as the ICJ and the ICC deal with globalization in terms of legal and criminal questions, the Global Compact addresses issues in the business world. The Global Compact—sometimes called the World Pact—began in 2000 as an opportunity for large corporations to come together and discuss globalization issues. Corporations that become members promise to make changes in their business practices to better align with the ten principles of the Global Compact. As of the beginning of 2015, over 12,000 corporate participants from around 145 countries around the world had joined.

One of the objectives of the Global Compact is to work for the abolition of child labor. Pictured here are two Nepali girls working in a brick factory in 2010.

PRINCIPLES OF THE GLOBAL COMPACT

Human Rights

- the support and respect of the protection of international human rights
- the refusal to participate or condone human rights abuses

Labor

- the support of freedom of association and the recognition of the right to collective bargaining
- the abolition of compulsory labor
- the abolition of child labor
- the elimination of discrimination in employment and occupation

Environment

- the implementation of a precautionary and effective program for environmental issues
- initiatives that demonstrate environmental responsibility
- the promotion of the diffusion of environmentally friendly technologies

Anticorruption

- the promotion and adoption of initiatives to counter all forms of corruption, including extortion and bribery

The principles of the Global Compact are similar to the goals laid out in the Charter of the United Nations. They include the support of human rights and anticorruption, as well as guidelines in the areas of labor and environmental practices.

Some human rights groups have been wary of the Global Compact, stating that the principles of the United Nations do not line up with the aims of large corporations. They fear the greed and the drive toward money-making often found in businesses could corrupt the United Nations and that some dishonest companies could use their membership in the Global Compact as a shield to protect their corrupt business practices. The United Nations, on the other hand, believes corporations can work in partnership with it to achieve the same goals and make the Earth a better place for all people.

Former United Nations Secretary-General Kofi Annan speaks with the media after the June 30, 2012, meeting of the Action Group for Syria at the United Nations Office in Geneva. After his term as UN secretary-general, Annan has continued to promote the United Nations and has continued to advocate for its reform.

As a global organization, the United Nations is very concerned with all aspects of globalization. With nearly all nations of the world as members, the United Nations can work with most of the world to create solutions for global problems. Organizations such as the ICJ, the ICC, and the Global Compact help the United Nations to end human rights violations and find ways to deal with other global issues.

Although the United Nations has many ideals, many of these principles have not been realized. In the near future, the United Nations has plans to strengthen the organization and make reforms to address problems within its own walls.

United Nations Reform

When Kofi Annan became secretary-general of the United Nations in 1997, he quickly presented the General Assembly with a package of reforms for the body. During his tenure, Annan proposed other changes to modernize the United Nations. Some of these have been carried out, such as consolidating three departments to create the Department of Economic and Social Affairs. Annan believes the United Nations must be constantly reevaluated and updated in order to function in the best way possible.

In 2005, Annan released a report called "In Larger Freedom: Toward Development, Security and Human Rights for All." In this report, Annan wrote:

> As the world's only universal body with a mandate to address security, development and human rights issues, the United Nations bears a special burden. As globalization shrinks distances around the globe and these issues become increasingly interconnected, the comparative advantages of the United Nations become ever more evident. So too, however, do some of its real weaknesses. From overhauling basic management practices and building a more transparent, efficient and effective United Nations system to revamping our major intergovernmental institutions so that they reflect today's world and advance the priorities set forth in the present report, we must reshape the Organization in ways not previously imagined and with a boldness and speed not previously shown.

STRONGER PEACEKEEPERS

In 2007, UN Secretary-General Ban Ki-moon outlined several reform proposals for the UN that were supported by the General Assembly. Among other things, the secretary-general proposed creating a High Representative for Disarmament Affairs and restructuring the UN's peacekeeping function.

"In Larger Freedom" was a five-year progress report on the Millennium Declaration of 2000, in which nations promised to meet certain specific Millennium Development Goals by 2015. In his statement to the General Assembly accompanying the release of the report, Annan said, "What is needed now is not more declarations or promises, but action to fulfill the promises already made."

The difficulty lies in getting 193 member countries of the United Nations to agree on actions to be taken and to work together to carry out these actions. Even though all these countries have signed the Charter of the United Nations and agree on the broad principles, they often have very different ideas about how these principles should be put into practice.

A Stronger United Nations

The size and scope of the United Nations means that it can be awkward and unwieldy when trying to act quickly and decisively. Committees study an issue and then report to other committees, which write reports and make presentations to still higher-level committees. Strengthening the United Nations means, in part, streamlining the processes required to act, so that things can be accomplished more quickly and easily.

One relatively recent UN reform has been a major renovation of the Commission on Human Rights. In the past, it had become a place where atrocities and human rights violations were too often overlooked. In 2006, the General Assembly established the Human Rights Council (UNHRC) to replace the commission. Made up of forty-seven member states, the council is a group of inter-governmental agencies within the UN that protect human rights around the globe.

One proposal to make the UN more effective is to update the membership of the Security Council to better reflect the modern world. Security Council reforms would probably include an increase in the number of permanent Council members to include countries such as Germany, Japan, or Brazil, as well as African countries. None of the new permanent members would have the veto power of the original members.

A boy rides his bike next to a ruined mosque in Azaz, Syria, May 2012, part of the destruction resulting from the Syrian Civil War, which began in 2010.

Taking Charge

Part of the job of the United Nations Human Rights Council is to monitor human rights' abuses around the globe. As a result, the council has created Commissions of Inquiry, fact-finding missions, and investigations in several countries.

In 2011, for example, it began looking at abuses in Syria, the site of a bloody civil war. In 2014, the council released its report blaming the Syrian government for mass atrocities against civilians. The council reported that fighting has destroyed many civilian areas. "Hundreds of civilians are dying each day as the fighting goes on with no regard to law or to conscience," said Paulo Pinheiro, chair of the Commission.

* * *

The world has become increasingly connected during the last century, and the United Nations, as a major global organization, must struggle to change and adapt to the world's changing needs. Often, the ideals of the United Nations have not been realized and good ideas have floundered in its own **bureaucracy**. Despite its failures, the United Nations has continued to try and make the world a better place for all people, meeting the challenges of globalization and using the benefits these connections have brought. To fully meet its goals, the United Nations will need the support of all the world's countries and leaders.

CHAPTER SIX

TEXT-DEPENDENT QUESTIONS

1. What is the Global Compact?

2. Where is the International Court of Justice based?

3. In what year did the ICC convict Thomas Lubanga Dyilo, founder and leader of the Union of Congolese Patriots?

RESEARCH PROJECTS

1. Create a visual presentation using charts and photographs showing how the world has become more globalized in the last hundred years. Remember to include captions explaining each chart and image.

2. Write a report on how the UN might help to protect religious and other cultural rights of indigenous peoples.

TIME LINE

1946	UN Commission on Human Rights is established.
	International Court of Justice is created.
1947	International Law Commission is formed.
1948	Universal Declaration of Human Rights is adopted.
1972	UN Conference on the Human Environment takes place in Stockholm, Sweden.
	United Nations Environmental Programme (UNEP) is founded.
1979	WHO declares smallpox eradicated.
1986	Special Rapporteur of the Commission on Human Rights on Freedom of Religion or Belief is appointed.
1992	UN Conference on Environment and Development takes place in Rio de Janeiro, Brazil (usually called the Earth Summit).
	United Nations Division for Sustainable Development (UNDSD) is founded.
Oct. 17, 1993	First annual International Day for the Eradication of Poverty takes place.
1995	World Summit for Social Development takes place in Copenhagen, Denmark.

1997	Kofi Annan becomes Secretary-General of the United Nations.
	The Kyoto Protocol calls for reductions in greenhouse gas emissions by 5.2 percent of 1990 levels.
1997–2006	United Nations Decade for the Eradication of Poverty.
2000	Millennium World Peace Summit of Religious and Spiritual Leaders.
	The Millennium Declaration sets out eight Millennium Development Goals to be met by 2015.
	Permanent Forum on Indigenous Issues is created.
	The Global Compact is created.
2002	International Poverty Center in Brasilia, Brazil, is created.
	International Criminal Court is established.
2006	The UN Human Rights Council (UNHRC) replaces the Commission on Human Rights.
2008	The Second United Nations Decade for the Eradication of Poverty begins.
2012	The ICC convicts Thomas Lubanga Dyilo, founder the leader of the Union of Congolese Patriots (UPC), of war crimes.

FURTHER RESEARCH

Books

Downie, David L., et al. *Climate Change: A Reference Handbook.* Santa Barbara, CA: ABC-CLIO, 2009.

Ellwood, Robert S., and Gregory D. Alles. *Encyclopedia of World Religions,* revised edition. New York: Facts On File, 2006.

Merino, Faith. *Human Rights.* New York: Facts On File, 2011.

United Nations at a Glance. New York: United Nations Publications, 2012.

Online Sources

The Global Compact: www.unglobalcompact.org/index.html

Global Issues: www.globalissues.org/

The Globalization Web site
www.sociology.emory.edu/globalization/

Human Rights Council
www.ohchr.org/EN/HRBodies/HRC/Pages/AboutCouncil.aspx

International Court of Justice
www.icj-cij.org/homepage/index.php?lang=en

International Criminal Court
www.icc-cpi.int/en_menus/icc/Pages/default.aspx

World Health Organization (WHO): www.who.int/en/

NOTE TO EDUCATORS: This book contains both imperial and metric measurements as well as references to global practices and trends in an effort to encourage the student to gain a worldly perspective. We, as publishers, feel it's our role to give young adults the tools they need to thrive in a global society.

SERIES GLOSSARY

abstain: not to vote for or against proposal when a vote is held.

Allies: the countries that fought against Germany in World War I or against the Axis powers in World War II.

ambassador: an official representative of one country to another country.

amendments: process of changing a legal document.

appeal: a formal request to a higher authority requesting a change of a decision.

appeasement: a deliberate attempt pacify a potentially troublesome nation.

arbitration: the process of resolving disputes through an impartial third party.

asylum: protection granted by a nation to someone who has left fled their country as a political refugee.

Axis: the alliance of Germany, Italy, and Japan that fought the allies in World War II.

blocs: groups of countries or political parties with the same goal.

bureaucracy: a complex system of administration, usually of a government or corporation.

capital: material wealth in the form of money or property.

civil law: law of a state dealing with the rights of private citizens.

coalition: in military terms, a group of nations joined together for a common purpose against a common enemy.

codification: the arrangement of laws into a systematic code.

Cold War: a largely nonviolent conflict between capitalist and communist countries following World War II.

compliance: conforming to a regulation or law.

conservation: preservation, management, and care of natural and cultural resources.

constitution: an official document outlining the rules of a system or government.

conventions: agreements between countries, less formal than treaties.

decolonization: the act of granting a colony its independence.

delegates: individuals chosen to represent or act on behalf of an organization or government.

demographic: characteristics of a human population.

diplomatic: having to do with international negotiations without resorting to violence.

disarmament: the reduction of a nation's supply of weapons or strength of its armed forces.

due process: the official procedures in legal cases required by law to ensure that the rights of all people involves are protected.

embargo: a government order limiting or prohibiting trade.

envoys: diplomats who act on behalf of a national government.

epidemic: a widespread occurrence of an infectious disease.

ethnic cleansing: the killing or imprisonment of an ethnic minority by a dominant group.

exchange rates: rates at which money of one country is exchanged the money of another.

extradition: the handing over by one government of someone accused of a crime in a different country for trial or punishment.

extremist: having to do with radical political or religious beliefs.

factions: smaller groups within larger groups that have opposing ideas.

fascist: relating to a system of government characterized by dictatorship, repression of opposition, and extreme nationalism.

flashpoints: areas of intense conflict and insecurity that often erupt into violent confrontation.

forgery: the act of making or producing an illegal copy of something.

free-market economy: economic system in which businesses operate without government control in matters such as pricing and wage levels.

genocide: systematic killing of all people from a national, ethnic, or religious group, or an attempt to do so.

globalization: the various processes that increase connections peoples of the world.

gross domestic product: total value of all goods and services produced within a country.

guerrilla: unorganized and small-scale warfare carried out by independent units.

human trafficking: the practice of seizing people against their will for the purpose of "selling" them for work, usually in the sex trade.

humanitarian: being concerned with or wanting to promote the well-being of other humans.

ideological: based on a specific system of beliefs, values, and ideas forming the basis of a social, economic, or political philosophy

indigenous: relating to the original inhabitants of an area or environment.

infrastructure: physical structures of a region, made up of roads, bridges, and so forth.

isolationism: the belief that a country should limit their involvement in the affairs of other countries.

mandate: an official instruction by an authority.

mediation: the process of resolving a dispute.

money laundering: the transferring of illegally obtained money through various businesses and accounts so as to hide it.

nationalists: people with an extreme sense of loyalty to their country.

nationalize: takeover by a government of a private business.

pandemic: a widespread epidemic in which a disease spreads to many countries and regions of the world.

per capita income: average amount earned by each individual in a country.

preamble: introduction, or opening words of a document.

precedent: established practice; a decision used as the basis of future decisions.

proliferation: the rapid spread of something.

propaganda: information or publicity put out by an organization or government to spread and promote a policy or idea.

protocols: preliminary memoranda often formulated and signed by diplomatic negotiators.

rapporteur: an official in charge of investigating and reporting to an agency, institution, or other entity.

ratification: the act of formally approving something.

referendum: a vote of the entire electorate on a question or questions put before it by the government or similar body.

reparation: compensation made by a nation defeated by others in a war.

sanction: a punishment imposed as a result of breaking a rule or law.

signatories: persons or governments who have signed a treaty and are bound by it.

sovereignty: self-rule, usually of a nation.

standard of living: the minimum amount of necessities essential to maintaining a comfortable life.

summit: a meeting between heads of government or other high-ranking officials.

sustainable: able to be maintained so that the resource is not depleted or damaged.

veto: the power of a person, country, or branch of government to reject the legislation of another.

INDEX

Ki-moon, Ban 17, 46, 49, 54, 74

Mexico 12, 14, 19
Middle East 12

natural disasters 40
Nicaragua 67, 68

outsourcing 17

piracy 9, 20
plague 36
pollution 22, 23, 24
poverty 30, 36, 40, 42, 43-50

reforestation 31

smallpox 35, 39
sovereignty 60
Sweden 25, 78

tsunami 39

United Nations
        Agenda 21 30, 31, 32
        Charter 15, 25, 46, 54, 71, 74
        Children's Fund (UNICEF) 40
        Commission on Human Rights 47, 59, 61, 74, 78
        Commitment to Global Peace 55, 56, 57
        Conference on Environment and Development (UNCED) 29, 78
        Conference on the Human Environment 25, 27, 78
        Conference on Trade and Development (UNTAD) 15
        Congress on the Preservation of Religious Diversity 56
        Convention on Biological Diversity 30, 31
        Coordination of Humanitarian Affairs (OCHA) 39, 40
        Council of Religious and Spiritual Leaders 55, 56
        Department of Economic and Social Affairs 73

PICTURE CREDITS

Page	Location	Archive/Photographer
8	Middle	Dreamstime/Pindiyath100
10	Bottom	Library of Congress/L. Prang & Co.
12	Top	Wikimedia Commons/Thelmadatter
13	Full page	Wikimedia Commons/Aude
14	Bottom	Wikimedia Commons/Jonathan McIntosh
16	Full page	Library of Congress/Bain News Service
19	Full page	Wikimedia Commons/DVIDSHUB
20	Bottom	iStock.com/Simon Moran
22	Middle	Wikimedia Commons/BriYYZ
24-25	Top	Library of Congress/Arthur Rothstein
26	Full page	Wikimedia Commons/Pöllö
27	Top	Wikimedia Commons/Osvaldo Gago
28	Bottom	Wikimedia Commons/Famartin
29	Top	Dreamstime/Pabkov
31	Top	Dollar Photo Club/fazon
34	Middle	Public Domain
37	Top	Wikimedia Commons/Navy Medicine
38	Middle	Wikimedia Commons/PO (Phot) Carl Osmond, MOD
39	Top	Wikimedia Commons/Thorkild Tylleskar
40	Bottom	Wikimedia Commons/U.S. Department of Agriculture
42	Middle	Dreamstime/Photochris
44	Bottom	Wikimedia Commons/BlueSalo
45	Top	Wikimedia Commons/USAID Africa Bureau
47	Top	Wikimedia Commons/ILRI, Stevie Mann
48	Bottom	Wikimedia Commons/Junkyardsparkle
50	Bottom	Wikimedia Commons/Christine Zenino
52	Middle	Wikimedia Commons/calflier001
54	Bottom	Wikimedia Commons/James Gordon
56	Top	Wikimedia Commons/Bernard Gagnon
57	Bottom	Dreamstime/Minyun Zhou
58	Bottom	Wikimedia Commons/Yourway-to-israel
59	Middle	Wikimedia Commons/Arnfinn Pettersen
60	Full page	Jupiter Images
62	Bottom	Dreamstime/Bbbar
64	Middle	Dreamstime/Tupungato
67	Top	Wikimedia Commons/National Archives and Records Administration
68	Bottom	Wikimedia Commons/Iamthestig
70	Middle	Wikimedia Commons/Krish Dulal
72	Top	Wikimedia Commons/US Mission in Geneva
75	Bottom	Dreamstime/Richard Harvey

BIOGRAPHIES

Author

SHEILA NELSON has written a number of educational books for young people. She lives in Rochester, New York, with her husband and children.

Series Advisor

BRUCE RUSSETT is Dean Acheson Professor of Political Science at Yale University and editor of the Journal of Conflict Resolution. He has taught or researched at Columbia, Harvard, M.I.T., Michigan, and North Carolina in the United States, and educational institutions in Belgium, Britain, Israel, Japan, and the Netherlands. He has been president of the International Studies Association and the Peace Science Society, and holds an honorary doctorate from Uppsala University in Sweden. He was principal adviser to the U.S. Catholic Bishops for their pastoral letter on nuclear deterrence in 1985, and codirected the staff for the 1995 Ford Foundation report, *The United Nations in Its Second Half Century*. He has served as editor of the *Journal of Conflict Resolution* since 1973. The twenty-five books he has published include *The Once and Future Security Council* (1997), *Triangulating Peace: Democracy, Interdependence, and International Organizations* (2001), *World Politics: The Menu for Choice* (8th edition 2006), and *Purpose and Policy in the Global Community* (2006).